First edition.

HURT

The First Boy Who Kissed Me

The first boy who kissed me held me down as tightly as he held his bicycle handles to avoid falling off.

The first boy who kissed me looked at me like he had just found a long lost toy-

he had that hope and wonder in his eyes.

The first boy who kissed me told me not to tell if I didn't want to get in trouble.

But, a few weeks later the words came out without me saying anything. I watched as tears ran down my father's face-

I had never seen him cry before.

The first boy who kissed me had stuffed his fingers into a confused and helpless version of me,

and it felt like he was trying to scrape the walls of a watermelon clean.

I push people away

I shut them out

I build a wall that I refuse to take down, for anyone

I hate myself for this

I want to be able to trust people, and believe them when they say

that they care about me

-I'm trying so hard to be ok

A list of lies I tell myself:

- He is a horrible person
- I don't care that he's gone
- I'm getting over him
- Eventually I'll move on
- I don't need or want to see him so it doesn't matter that I won't
- He left - and I'm okay with that
- I don't miss him at all

& you'll run away,

without ever leaving your bedroom.

You haven't cried in 18 days,

even though you're always crying.

The worst part about love leaving is that you don't go with it,

you just attend the funeral and visit the grave every time you're drunk on your own sadness.

& it feels like you're always wasted.

Toybox

He never wanted to play with me

So when he asked me to go hide

I was excited

I ran around in a hurry hearing his voice in the distance

I found the perfect spot

It was one of my favorite spots

The toy box he had that I had wanted

It was cool, I thought

It had come white as could be, shiny, covered in animals

When I opened his closet to hide, the darkness inside was petrifying

I climbed onto that toy box anyways

The white was brown. The top was peeling

Hard and sharp, stabbing into my leg

I should've known what was coming,

The omens were everywhere

But how could a 5 year old possibly ever predict this

what scares me the most is that I'll wake up one day and forget my own name,

but still remember yours

I was raised to see holes in walls and doors as something that just happens.

I was raised by voices always being a little bit louder.

I was raised to take all the hits like a punching bag.

I was raised being taught the world is horrible,

we don't get what we want

and life is unfair.

I was raised to know that pain isn't just physical.

I was raised having my imaginary friend be a close companion,

a play-mate.

I was raised to have felt real life at age 6,

to know that the world is much darker than it seems

and crueler than anyone expected.

-I was raised to grow-up.

I guess I wanted to be ruined a little more than I wanted to be loved;

after all,

I loved you even while you were ripping me apart.

That says a lot more about me than it does you

when all I could feel was my heart starting to rot,

becoming as shriveled as yours,

that's when I knew you weren't good for me anymore

-toxic

REALIZING

If you're going to love me, love me deeply

If you break my heart, then shatter it

If you're going to care, take care of every part of me

If you decide not to hold on, then let me fall

If you're going to stay, stay forever

If you want to leave, than do it today

-my mind makes everything turn into all or nothing

I came home smelling like rain, cigarette smoke, & teenage love

I thought things were gonna change, I felt ecstatic

I smiled and stuck my hand in my pocket where you had rested your fingers after telling me that you were 22 degrees and I was the sun and I could melt you with my fingertips

I came home smelling like vodka, tears, and vomit

and when I looked in the mirror I noticed the way your sweater dangled off me

I came home trying to put back together the necklace you gave me;

the clasp was broken but I twisted the chain around my fingers and held it tighter.

I came home smelling like a thunderstorm and breakup songs,

things I should have said but never did and things I said that I shouldn't have ever let fly out of my mouth.

My mom just stared at me.

-You're ruining me

Toybox II

You shut the door behind yourself

And climbed onto the toybox across from me, you had jeans on

I had my pink dress with the strawberry over my heart

My legs were bare

The plastic was hurting

I wanted to get out

It was my turn to count

You told me to stay

You pulled your jeans down

You made me sit cross legged

Hands. Fear. Pain. Darkness

That's all I could think of

I was treated like a fish

Plunged into and gutted

I was playing with your hair even though you hate that and you told me to stop so I did, but then you were so angry with me. You sat up quickly and just gave me this look - it's hard to describe but it definitely wasn't a look of happiness and love.

We just sat there staring at each other, I apologized, started holding back tears and….. you scoffed at me with the most disgusted look on your face. It devastated me.

I started grabbing at you but you pulled away. You stood, and just looked at me with confusion in your eyes and somehow I knew that the confusion was about how you could have ever loved a train wreck like me and I physically ached.

I then knew what was coming.

You looked me in my eyes and took a step back as you shook your head, you grabbed at your hair as if you couldn't believe that you had ever let yourself love me.

"I can't, I don't, I don't know how I can love you. I don't anymore." You said it with such confidence that it made me sick.

I rushed to the bathroom and threw up the words I wanted to say to you. I sat up from the toilet as a storm of tears left my eyes and then woke up;

realizing it was a dream but acknowledging that

even though the event wasn't real

the fact that you were gone

was.

You.

You were like a ripped painting, beautiful even with all of your tears.

You had a smoking habit that crusted my lungs, now they're raisins.

You took from me like I was a medicine cabinet that had everything you needed to heal your damaged soul; you took even after I had nothing more to give.

But, you weren't empty anymore, I'd mended your soul like we both wanted, but suddenly I was the empty one.

I'm sorry for trying to fix you, I guess I've never really known what to do with my hands

I ended up seeing myself digging through your insides forcing myself to try to reassemble the broken pieces,

you never asked me to do that.

I'm sorry that I held onto us when seemingly there was nothing left to hold on to.

I think I just needed to feel something and you were there.

I'm sorry for writing metaphors about love, heartbreak, and tearing our love apart all over your bedroom wall.

I bet a fresh coat of paint would cover them up.

This is an apology letter,

to the both of us

for how long it took me to move on.

I used to go to bed screaming your name into my pillow.

I would cry until I was choking and grasping at my chest, trying to take out my heart so I wouldn't have to feel. I didn't want to feel your touch lingering on my arm even though it was weeks since you bothered coming around.

Then suddenly it's months later, but it feels like years.

and my heart is accidentally broken from me slamming the door too hard as I left.

I know you told me you loved me, but there are still imprints on the palms of my hands from the pills

My body is still shaking even though the heating bill was paid this month

There are still blood stains on my wrists. There are still blood stains on my favorite sweater from when you ripped my heart out like it was nothing

My hair still smells like the bath water from when I tried to drown myself in the tub; but my toe slipped and unplugged the drain which washed everything away except for me

I'm so alone

My bed feels empty because my ghosts have been gone for a few months and I'm starting to miss them. I think I've started pretending that they're still here

And I'm not even sure if there's room for you anymore

I know you said you loved me, but you should probably stay gone.

To the next that decides to love me:

1. I watched love crumble often. Forgive me when I try to do the same to us
2. I was told I know pain a little too well, some days it might devastate me but just know I've been trying to heal
3. There's a chance I'll tear a hole into your heart to try to protect mine, I did it to the one before
4. I've seen the darkness of this world, but that's not what makes me. I'm slowly learning that there's more than *just* my pain
5. I'll use metaphors too much; more than you've ever heard
6. Some say I'm what holds things together, but more say I'm the best at tearing them apart

FALLING

everybody else isn't you and it turns out that that is a problem for me

You're taking over my thoughts, slowly, yet intrusively.

I look forward to the days and nights now, when I once dreaded anything that involved me being out of bed and breathing.

The butterflies slam against my stomach so hard that I feel nauseous;

but so excited that I'm finally getting some of you into my system

Not only do I feel like I want you, but part of me acts like I need you.

-You're like a drug to me

My first kiss with you is the only first kiss I need to remember when the world ends, I will scream out into the chaos that I'm in love with you

I didn't even realize I was in love with him at first,

but then I noticed how his voice wasn't just that background noise anymore,

it was something that I searched for and wanted to hear.

I noticed how I could spend every free moment I had just looking at him

because his smile and laugh made me feel warmer than the 98 degree sun outside.

I noticed that his eyes weren't the same color-one was green and one blue;

they pulled me in more than I thought was possible.

And suddenly he wasn't just that one guy anymore,

but the reason I started feeling the love I never thought I would know.

I started to wonder why I was ever unhappy before,

because the universe managed to create him

and I was lucky enough to know him in this life.

He became the thing that pulled me out of the water I was drowning in.

That's when I realized I was in love.

Every time I kiss you it feels like I'm watching fireworks,

or a sunset,

the start of fall,

traffic lights reflecting off the rain on the road

Lately, there hasn't been an hour that's passed where I don't think about how your lips make me feel when they're on mine

-You're all the things that bring me joy combined into one

Please know that I love you more than even I can begin to understand:

If you ripped my chest open you could find everything I love about you on the inseam of my heart

If you could see how my insides light up like the glow in the dark stars I used to have stuck on my ceiling every time I hear your laugh

Or how every time I look into your eyes and see one blue one green while studying the flecks of golden brown in each my heart swells and I fall in love a little bit more

Or how your voice wraps around my bones and keeps them from shivering like they did every time I would fall asleep

How the tips of your fingers warm my very core

How the sound of you breathing into my ear is my new favorite soundtrack

How I want to live in your rib cage and fall asleep to the sound of your blood running,

your lungs inhaling and exhaling,

your heart pumping and giving you life, which gives me life

How I crave to fall asleep in the crook of your neck for the rest of my days

How honey pours from your mouth with every kind word said

How your lips are the galaxy and you taste like the stardust my soul has unknowingly been needing

How I could drown our Earth in everything that I feel for you

-I Know I Love You,

But I Think I Might Need You

I was terrified.

I got used to flinching and faking.

The ache in me was so undeniably fresh and raw.

I had craved you, in every way imaginable.

But how was I supposed to know if you felt the same?

I had seeds of distrust planted into my core.

I was overthinking it,

I knew this because each small touch

held an enormous amount of sincerity.

I could not believe

that the person I wanted most

was being this tender.

Your skin was more gentle on mine

then I knew was possible.

I was used to sandpaper and fire.

I ingrained the memory into my skin

because you were loving me in a way

I didn't know I needed to be loved,

but yet it was the exact way I needed.

HEALING & GROWING

Why is it that I feel like I can only write about the demons that haunt me,

the things that hurt me the most.

Why can I vomit up those words with finesse,

but struggle to breathe when I even **think** about the words for the things that bring me the happiness I spent so long *desperately* searching for.

I want to find the words to explain how I never thought I'd find any light

in my once blackened soul,

but then I did.

I'm gonna hold onto it for as long as I can.

I feel such hope every time you embrace me.

I feel safe in your arms, I don't want to leave this because

I could never stop loving you.

If I ever lost you I would be in agony.

Heartbreak.

Because my heart now knows comfort.

Fullness.

Unconditional love that is fathomless.

You're like a lit candle in a dark room,

or the moon at 2 A.M.

when the sky is at its darkest.

Moving Forward,

I know that I won't have to question everything,

every late night home,

every text message,

every hangout with "friends".

It took me a long time,

but I can finally relax,

I can finally trust undoubtedly,

I can believe the words that are spoken to me.

Moving forward,

and thanks to you,

I know that loyalty exists;

and that I deserve it.

I would go to that park a few blocks from your place.

Just to sit on the swings and stare forward at nothing.

I felt so broken every time I was there.

I always thought you could be what brought me that happiness,

the happiness that my brain had been starved of.

Oh man, how naive I was.

Admittedly, I still am time and again.

But, to think that someone else was going to "heal" me was the most naive I've ever been.

Nobody came to my rescue in those moments, especially not you.

-I had to learn to be okay with myself

before anything else.

I never wanted children, I know everybody says that.

But I truly didn't want to bring anything dependent on me into my life.

I was so scared that I wouldn't do it right, that I *couldn't* be the thing someone else needed.

Then I heard that first cry and felt that warmth against my chest.

The type of love that doesn't have to have time to grow, it's just there.

Already so fulfilling and intense.

I never wanted kids, but I'm so damn happy that I've been blessed beyond belief

Nobody looked at me,

in my most desperate and broken times,

and thought to themselves, "Gorgeous."

I thought there could be someone,

but it wasn't romantic the way I had dreamed about.

It deteriorated us.

Nobody ever picked up my shattered pieces and glued them
back together.

I couldn't even do it to myself in those times.

The bad news is that nobody comes to the rescue.

The good news is that you can rescue yourself.

If my heart was made from glass you could smash it with a hammer, shattering it.

If it was a flower you could let it wither and wilt

You could pour gasoline over it, throw a match on top

You could beat it to a bloody pulp

You could rip it out of me and take the life from it,

If that's what you needed

No matter what you do to it, it will still beat for you.

-being a mother

All those with their scraped knuckles,

blood-stained hearts,

and loves that ripped through them like a hurricane

weren't thoroughly honest.

They romanticize the hurt,

I

romanticized the hurt.

I don't want to do that anymore.

I don't want to romanticize the days that made me want to

smash the mirror.

Or the blues and purples on my heart

from the bruising of false hope,

and the lover who didn't love me back.

Instead,

I want to romanticize the love that's as sweet

as natural honey.

Zero hurricanes; no pain.

But the love that is so wonderful that you get built from within yourself.

The love that helps you make it through the bad days.

In reality,

there isn't any beauty in cigarette butts burning your shaky fingertips.

The beauty is in sugar falling from your fingers,

the day you find happiness,

the healing.

Printed in Great Britain
by Amazon